YOU BRING OUT THE ANIMAL IN ME
GAMES FOR TWO

© 1986, 1993, 2004 Arkas, Greece

Translation: Ingrid Behrmann

Distribution:
7, Gravias Str., 106 78 Athens, Greece
210.38.07.689 - fax: 210.38.10.892
w w w . p r o t o p o r i a . g r
www.arkas.gr

1

2

3

GAMES FOR TWO

by Azkas

Translation
INGRID BEHRMANN

grammata

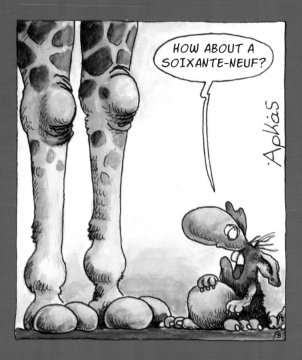

9

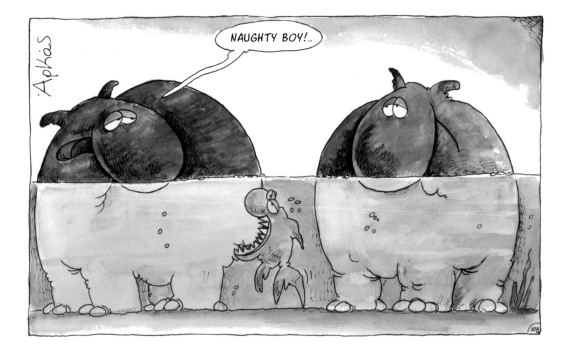

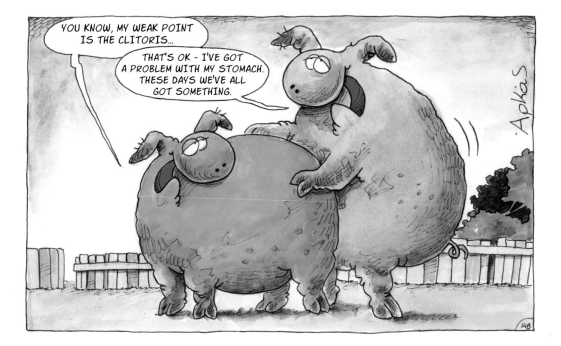

YOU
BRING OUT
THE ANIMAL
IN ME!..

YOU BRING OUT THE ANIMAL IN ME!..

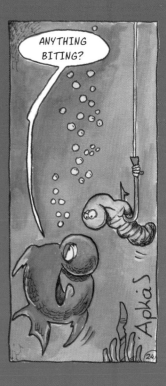

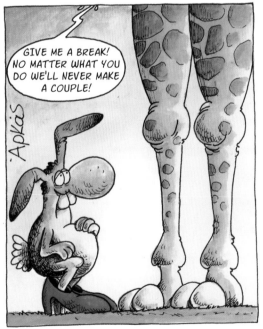

YOU BRING OUT THE ANIMAL IN ME!..

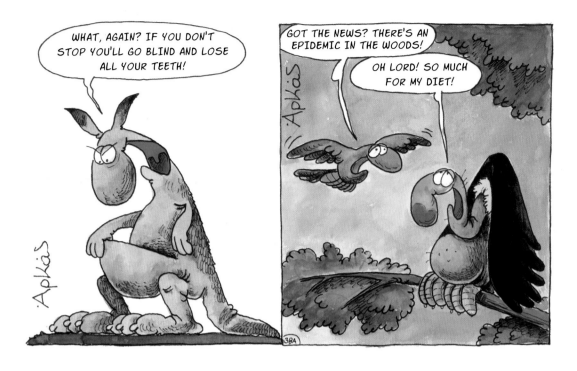

YOU
BRING OUT
THE ANIMAL
IN ME!...

45

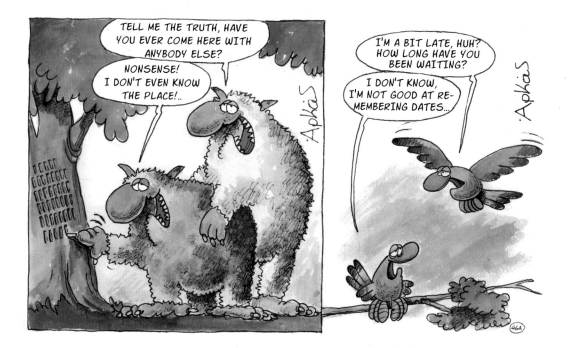

YOU BRING OUT THE ANIMAL IN ME!..

YOU BRING OUT THE ANIMAL IN ME!..

60

YOU BRING OUT THE ANIMAL IN ME!..

THIS CAN'T GO ON!
I'VE GOT TO BREAK UP
WITH THAT OSTRICH!

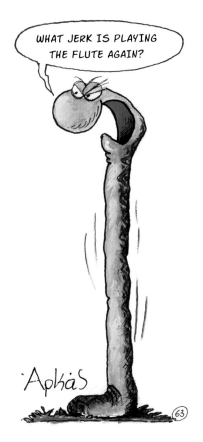